He Came

An Illustrated Family Christmas Reader

He Came

An Illustrated Family Christmas Reader

Joanne Jung

Illustrations by Gary Alexander

He Came
An Illustrated Family Christmas Reader
© GlossaHouse, LLC 2025

All rights reserved. No part of this book may be reproduced or transmitted in any form or by any means, electronic or mechanical, including photocopying or recording, or by means of any information storage or retrieval system, except as may be expressly permitted by the 1976 Copyright Act or in writing from the publisher. Requests for permission should be addressed in writing to the following:

GlossaHouse, LLC
110 Callis Circle
Wilmore, KY 40309
www.GlossaHouse.com

He Came
An Illustrated Family Christmas Reader
by Joanne Jung
Illustrated by Gary Alexander

ISBN: 978-1-63663-137-0

1. Jesus Christ—Nativity—Meditations. 2. Christmas—Religious aspects—Christianity. 3. Bible stories, New Testament. 4. Families—Religious life.

The fonts used to create this work are available from: www.linguistsoftware.com/lgku.htm

Cover design by Lisa C. Terris

Text Layout by Lisa C. Terris and Andrew J. Coutras
Interior book design by Andrew J. Coutras

This book is dedicated to the LORD and to his people. May Christ followers continue to be moved in humble awe at Jesus' coming and compelled to share his story.

He Came: An Illustrated Family Christmas Reader

He Came is based on the Christmas narrative from God's Word. It is filled with biblical truths that highlight the events surrounding the birth of Christ. The content of this book is framed using a simple alphabet book format. Do not let the simplicity of the A-Z order keep you from experiencing the awe of the Christmas story. Each letter presents a focal point of the narrative, which is expanded upon with brief yet informative comments. These entries unpack historical background or context, a theological concept, or even sometimes the common use of a letter from the Greek alphabet. The Scripture references on every page ensure the biblical accuracy of the text. Set in stunning watercolor paintings, each page will encourage readers and listeners alike to engage in conversations that foster knowing God and his Word.

A is for the Angel

The biblical words that are typically translated "angel" mean "messenger." An angel brought the divine birth announcement: Jesus is born. When angels appear in the Bible, people respond with astonishment and fear. Thus, their messages often begin with, as does this one, "Fear not." The angel continues, "for behold, I bring you good news of great joy that will be for all the people. For unto you is born this day in the city of David a Savior, who is Christ the Lord. And this will be a sign for you: you will find a baby wrapped in swaddling cloths and lying in a manger" (Luke 2:10-12).

Angels are powerful and intelligent spiritual beings, but do not seek attention for themselves. They are sent from God, obey his commands (Psalm 103:20), and minister to his people (Psalm 91:11; Hebrews 1:14). Angels bear witness to God by providing guidance, help, and encouragement. Though some spiritual beings are described as having sets of wings: seraphim with three pairs (Isaiah 6:2) and cherubim with two pairs of wings (Ezekiel 10:21), angels do not appear to have wings when encountering human beings. Rather, they look like human beings (e.g., Judges 13:6; Mark 16:5), and can appear shining and glorious (Acts 10:30).

Some angels have names and have a high rank or authority. Michael, an archangel (Daniel 10:13, 21; 12:1; Jude 1:9), commands God's army in victory (Revelation 12:7-9). The angel Gabriel announces to Mary that she will be the recipient of God's favor in the call to give birth to the Messiah (Luke 1:26-37).

B is for Bethlehem of Judea

Bethlehem means "(store)house of bread" (*beth* means house and *lehem* means bread in Hebrew) and is located in the hill country of Judea, about six miles south/southwest of Jerusalem, the home of the religious and political elite of Israel. Jerusalem would have been an expected birthplace for Jesus, a child with such regal majesty, but instead, he was born in Bethlehem. This was the hometown of Ruth and Boaz (Ruth 1:19, 2:4), great-grandparents to King David (Matthew 1:5-6).

More than 800 years before Jesus was born, the minor prophet Micah foretold that this tiny and insignificant town of Bethlehem would be the birthplace of the coming promised Messiah. This new king would rise to save Israel (Micah 5:2-4).

In his gospel, Luke refers to Bethlehem as the city of David because it was the birthplace of Israel's most beloved king (Luke 2:4). It was also the hometown of Joseph, the husband of Mary. Joseph, who was from the royal line of David (Matt 1:16) but living in the northern city of Nazareth, had to travel with Mary 90 miles in three days to his ancestral home of Bethlehem in order to register for the Roman census (Luke 2:1-5).

C is for Caesar Augustus

Who Ruled the Roman World of That Day

Caesar Augustus was given the name Octavian at birth. He was a grand-nephew and adopted son of Julius Caesar, so he inherited the name Caesar, becoming Caesar Octavian. He brought an end to civil war and ushered in Roman peace, or *Pax Romana*. This was considered "the gospel" (meaning "good news") of peace but was conditioned on Roman terror, conquest, and bloodshed.

He accepted the title Augustus, meaning "exalted" or "majestic." This was his attempt to set himself up as a god. As the first true Roman emperor, monuments declared and celebrated him as the political "savior" of the Roman world, having established stability and relative tranquility that would extend more than two centuries after his reign (from 27 BC to 14 AD). It was during Caesar Augustus' rule of the Roman Empire that Jesus was born. As Caesar, Augustus could order censuses to be taken to count the population, levy taxes, and for military assessment purposes. Augustus called for just such a census of the entire Roman world, and that brought Mary and Joseph to Bethlehem.

God accomplishes his divine plan through this unknowing ruler and his decree for official data collection, fulfilling the prophecy of the Messiah's birth in Bethlehem (Micah 5:2).

D is for the Dream of Joseph

Dreams are considered one way God communicated directly to people. They are found in both the Old Testament and the New Testament.

Joseph was a righteous man who was faithful to the law. Being engaged to a woman who was pregnant would bring shame to this godly man. In an effort to shield Mary from disgrace or even from being stoned as an apparent adulteress, Joseph secretly planned on divorcing her. In a dream, the angel commands him to "not be afraid"(Matthew 1:20-25). He was not to fear the stigma he would experience from Mary's pregnancy but instead was assured of God's plan. He is then told of the child miraculously conceived by the Holy Spirit. In response to this dream, Joseph takes Mary as his wife and becomes Jesus' earthly father.

This dream was the first of three divine communications to Joseph, which included the command for Joseph to flee to Egypt with the new mother and child (Matthew 2:13-15) and later, the command to return to Israel (Matthew 2:19-23). Similarly, the Magi from the east were warned in a dream to return to their own country by another route, thus avoiding a perilous journey by escaping Herod's wrath (Matthew 2:12).

E is for Elizabeth

The Mother of John the Baptist

Elizabeth was an older cousin of Mary, Jesus' mother. She was married to Zechariah, who served as a priest in Israel, but she was also from the honored priestly line. Both were righteous in God's sight, and both suffered the heartbreak of being childless. One day, during Zechariah's one-week long service in the temple, the angel Gabriel surprised him with an announcement that Elizabeth, who was far too old to have children, would bear a son. This baby was to be named John, even though it was customary that a son would bear his father's name. John would be the forerunner to Jesus' first coming.

When Mary visits the very pregnant Elizabeth, the baby within her jumps in her womb as if to welcome the unborn child Mary is carrying. When Elizabeth, filled with the Holy Spirit, proclaims to Mary, "Blessed are you among women, and your child will be blessed! How could this happen to me, that the mother of my Lord should come to me? the mother of my Lord," (Luke 1:42-43) she becomes the first person to confess Jesus as the Lord.

The intertestamental period that occurred between the Old Testament and the New Testament is known as the Four-hundred Years of Silence when Israel did not hear from God through the prophets, who had characteristically delivered messages of hope. Malachi, the last of the Old Testament prophets, foretells the coming of both God's messenger, John the Baptist, and Jesus (Malachi 3:1). John the Baptist, Elizabeth's son, is the last prophet as well as the forerunner, the one who prepares the way for the Messiah. He introduces Jesus as "the Lamb of God, who takes away the sins of the world!" (John 1:29).

F is for Frankincense, Gold, and Myrrh

Frankincense was one of three gifts presented to the infant king of the Jews and was a highly prized, fragrant substance used in worship. It was the only incense permitted on the temple altar and was associated with divinity (Exodus 30:34-38). Gold, as the most precious and rare metal, was a symbol of wealth and royal power. Myrrh, a treasured aromatic resin, was used as a perfume, a painkiller, an anointing oil, in incense, and to cover the smell of decay in the embalming process.

The gift-bearing Magi were gentile astrologers or sages of eastern wisdom who followed a star, which shone brilliantly. "At its rising" may indicate its mysterious appearance heralding the Christ child. One astrological explanation is that the star was actually an angel sent to announce and guide the Magi. The Magi traveled a long and dangerous journey from the east in search of the one born "king of the Jews" (Matthew 2:1-2).

Though three Magi are often depicted because of the three gifts given, there were probably up to twelve who traveled together in a caravan that included servants and guards. They were among the first gentile worshipers to search for and find the "child" Jesus, visiting him in a house (Matthew 2:11). This may indicate that Jesus was a toddler at the time.

The Magi's intent was to pay homage to the king of a ruling country and knew there was something very special about the One to whom they fell on their knees and worshiped. God protected these Magi, warning them in a dream not to return to Herod and to instead leave for their own country by a different route (Matthew 2:12).

G is for

"Glory to God in the Highest"

"Glory to God in the highest heaven and peace among those with whom he is pleased" was proclaimed by a supernova of angelic hosts filling the night sky. This public declaration of God's glory—a hymn of praise highlighting his majesty and fame—includes his initiative to extend his favor. Here, the shepherds are given an earthly sneak peek of God's glory (Luke 2: 9-13) both in the audible angelic praise that happens in heaven and the visual illumination of God's glory that shone around them.

In the first century, the Romans understood peace to mean people being subject and obedient to their oppressive rule and threat of violence. God is the source of real, true, and lasting peace. The peace that Jesus brings (Luke 2:14) stands in contrast to Roman peace. Jesus as the Prince of Peace (Isaiah 9:6) enables restored relationships between God and sinful people. The peace of God and peace with God is now available to all. This is why the angels cosmically announced His glory.

God's glory is most visible and real in the person of Jesus Christ (John 1:14; Heb 1:3), who is the exact representation of God because he is God. Jesus is fully human while at the same time fully God. He shows God's glory as he establishes his kingdom reign on earth and in our hearts.

H is for Herod the Great

Herod the Great was given the title "King of the Jews," though he did not have the ancestry to rule over the Jews nor was he from Judah, the tribe from which Israel's ruler would come (Genesis 49:8-12). He was appointed king of Judea by Caesar Augustus in 39 BC and was known for his great and extensive building projects, especially the Second Temple in Jerusalem. His paranoia, however, led him to mastermind brutal acts of murder, even against members of his own immediate family.

When the Magi inquired of the birthplace of the "king of the Jews," Herod didn't know how to answer them. He summoned his chief priests and teachers of the law who knew the Scriptures and was told the new king would be born in Bethlehem of Judea (Matthew 2:1-8; Micah 5:2). Suspicious of this new "king of the Jews," Herod feared for his own royal reign. He secretly meets with the Magi and sends them to Bethlehem, commanding them to return to him and confirm this new king's birth, so that he himself could "go and worship" him.

Herod's deceptive ploy was foiled when the Magi, informed through a dream, outwitted him by not returning. In a rage, knowing where to direct his plot against the would-be king, he attempted to eliminate Jesus by issuing the edict to massacre all the baby boys two years old and under living in Bethlehem (Matthew 2:16). This devastates this small and close-knit town of Bethlehem.

I is for Immanuel

    The gospel writer, Matthew, quotes Isaiah 7:14 where the Hebrew word *'immanu 'el* means "God with us." Isaiah's prophecy is directed to Ahaz, a compromising and hypocritical king of Judah, the southern kingdom of Israel's Divided Kingdom period. He decides not to trust God and does not represent the line of David well. Isaiah foretells that God will be faithful to his promise to be present with the sons of David and provide deliverance for his people. This deliverance will come in his promised Son, who would be called Immanuel - God with us. The name Immanuel is used only once in the New Testament and represents Jesus' God-given role of bringing God's presence to mankind. God knows what every human being needs because of our rebellion against him. Instead of giving up on us, he provides a way for each of us to be in a right relationship with him and receive life purpose and unconditional love. It would be through the forgiveness found in Jesus' completed work. That's why he came.

    This exalted fulfillment is found in Matthew's use of Immanuel as a representative name for Jesus (Matthew 1:23), signifying his deity as God incarnate; a divine-human person living among other humans. He came to reflect God's compassion and rule, saving his people from their sins (Matthew 1:21). In God's protecting presence is joy, rest, and strength. As "God with us," Jesus embodies the presence of God, a theme found throughout God's word. God is with us because of Jesus.

J is for the Name of the God-man

Jesus

When Joseph was instructed by an angel in a dream to take Mary as his wife, he was also told to name her son Jesus (Matthew 1:21, 25). Jesus' conception by the Holy Spirit and his natural birth through Mary unites human nature to the divine person of Christ.

Through a series of transliterations, the name Jesus comes to us from his original Hebrew name, *Yeshua*, then through Greek, to Latin, then Germanic, and finally to English. He was officially named Jesus eight days after his birth, when he was also circumcised in keeping with Jewish law (Luke 2:21; Genesis 17:12).

The angel declaring to Mary that she will bear the Son of the Most High attests to Jesus' divine nature. While Jesus is fully God, the exact representation of God's being (Hebrews 1:1-3), he is, at the same time, fully human, acquainted with the total human experience. He precisely fulfills Old Testament messianic prophecies as the Son of God. As if that wasn't enough, Jesus, the long-awaited Messiah from the royal line of King David, now lives among and within his people. The angel's message that "he will save his people from their sins" (Matthew 1:21) declares that God incarnate, God in human flesh, came to give life to humanity. It was not that Jesus was merely like God but that he actually is God—and as God, he came.

K is for the King of Kings

Jesus is declared king at his birth (Matthew 2:2-6; Psalm 2:7-9; Micah 5:2). The Davidic kingship was firmly established through the Old Testament. In the aftermath of the exile from their land and the end of the Davidic dynasty, however, the people continued to hope expectantly for the One who would rule the earth with justice and equity (Isaiah 11:1-5) and whose kingdom would never end.

The four Gospels ("Gospel means "good news"), written by Matthew, Mark, Luke, and John, are ancient biographies of Christ. One of the primary goals of the Gospels is to draw readers' attention to the kingdom of God, answering questions about its king and describing what his never-ending rule is like. They prove that Jesus is the Messiah, the One who provides salvation from sin, humanity's greatest need. All human beings experience the pain and suffering of sin and its consequences. So, in his love, God provided the true Savior and King whose transcendent power, majesty, and authority to forgive and redeem establishes his worthiness to rule the earth and over all other earthly kings.

There's nothing extraordinary or spectacular about Jesus' birthplace or childhood. As an infant child, he did all the things babies characteristically do. As the Anointed King, Jesus was specifically sent from God. With the numerous prophecies about a restored Davidic kingdom throughout the Old Testament, people were expecting a king. What was intriguing and mysterious about Jesus' claims was that this King was God himself.

L is for Light of the World

The image of God as Light appears in both the first and last books of the Bible. In Genesis 1:3, God speaks light into existence. In the future there will be no need for the sun or moon because God's glory supplies light to the new Jerusalem and Jesus is the lamp (Revelation 21:23). There are over 200 references to God as Light throughout Scripture.

Darkness represents danger. At the time of Jesus' birth, the darkness of social injustice and self-interest characterized the political and religious leaders. King Herod ruled from Jerusalem with violence, self-interest, and corruption stemming from his personal agendas. In the same way, political feuds existed between various religious sects like the Pharisees and Sadducees, Zealots, and Essenes. They were, however, united in opposing Herod's rule. Amid such turmoil, the leaders of Jerusalem felt compelled to preserve their power and authority at any cost.

Against this backdrop of darkness and sin, the Messiah brings God's darkness-defeating presence (John 8:12) and his divine forgiveness (Acts 26:17-18). The coming of Jesus is the dawning of light (John 1:5). He is the Light of the world, who was foretold in the Old Testament (Isaiah 9:2, 42:6-7; Numbers 24:17) and revealed in the New Testament (Matthew 4:16). Jesus gives hope to the world because God transfers believers from the domain of darkness to the kingdom of his Son (Colossians 1:13), into his marvelous light (1 Peter 2:9).

M is for Mary, Jesus' Mother

Like many Jewish girls of the first century, Mary was likely pledged to be married at around age 12 and would be married the year after. The angel Gabriel appears to Mary and informs her in a most unique and unusual way that she would give birth to the Son of the Most High, Jesus. He would be conceived without any involvement from a man (Luke 1:26-38). Mary's response reveals her knowledge of the Old Testament Scriptures, as she praises him for his faithfulness, covenant promises, protection, and salvation.

In Luke 1:46-55, Mary is included in the genealogy of Jesus that is recorded in Matthew 1. It shows the physical line of Jesus starting from Abraham, highlighting Jesus' relationship with Israel. Women were not typically included in Jewish genealogies, but Matthew includes five. Four of the women were Gentiles; the King of the Jews would have Gentile ancestry. God's kingdom and Jesus' kingship is truly inclusive.

Jesus' genealogy in Luke 3:23-38 depicts his royal or legal lineage tracing back to Adam and thus relating Jesus to all of humankind. Both Joseph and Mary come from King David's line, Solomon and Nathan, respectively, and converge at Jesus. Prophecy declared that the Messiah would come from the line of David. Through Mary and Joseph, God fulfilled that prophecy undeniably. Jesus, the son of David as the son of Mary and Joseph, is the Son of God, the Messiah.

N is for Nazareth

Never mentioned in the Old Testament, Nazareth was a secluded, obscure agricultural village in the southern part of Galilee, over 1,100 feet above sea level and situated between the Mediterranean Sea and the Sea of Galilee. Though off the beaten path, it was still accessible from the main trade routes and thus not cut off from the world around it. The area supplied fish and grain, staples of the Jewish diet, nevertheless, it was not a highly respected region, and its residents were despised by Jews in Jerusalem. The unlikely town of Nazareth, even more obscure than Bethlehem, is God's choice over Jerusalem for the angel Gabriel to announce the birth of Messiah. The God-man would be raised in Nazareth. And because people did not have surnames in ancient times, he would be known as Jesus of Nazareth.

The fifty to sixty acres of Nazareth housed approximately five-hundred relatively poor residents. Its size and population were rather insignificant compared to Jerusalem. Though many Gentiles lived in Galilee, most residents were Jewish. Homes in Nazareth were mostly built in the same simple style. It was to this village of Nazareth that the angel Gabriel came to this divinely favored teenage girl who was pledged to be married and told her that she would be the mother of Jesus.

Jesus' mother, Mary, lived in Nazareth (Luke 1:26-27), and Jesus' adoptive father, Joseph, resided in Nazareth as well. Though Joseph may have expected to return to his ancestral home of Bethlehem when they escaped from Egypt after Jesus was born, he submits to God's direction to settle in Nazareth (Matthew 2:13-23). Lowly Nazareth is where Jesus grows up.

O is for "Out of Egypt"

Upon receiving urgent directions from an angel through a dream, Joseph took his young family and escaped from Bethlehem at night to the safety and sanctuary of Egypt, about eighty miles away. Egypt was friendly to the Jews and provided shelter for Jewish refugees. A large Jewish population was established there. Egypt was outside of Herod's jurisdiction, far enough away from his paranoia, anger, and terror. After no more than a year, Joseph was informed by the angel of the Lord in yet another dream that Herod had died and that it was safe to return to Israel (Matthew 2:19-21). The family traveled out of Egypt" to Israel and settled in Nazareth.

God provided an historic exodus of his people from the bondage and slavery of Egypt. Hosea 11:1 clearly refers to this past event. Because Jesus epitomizes and fulfills Israel's history, Matthew applies Hosea's phrase to Jesus in his Gospel. As Israel is God's son who was brought out of Egypt centuries earlier in the context of Pharoah's hatred, so also Jesus is God's Son brought out of Egypt into the Promised Land in the context of Herod's hatred (Exodus 4:22; Matthew 2:13-15).

P is for the Prophecies

of Simeon and Anna in the Temple

In obedience to the Law, Joseph and Mary brought eight-day-old Jesus to the temple for consecration (Luke 2:21-24). Their sacrifice of two turtledoves, rather than a lamb, indicates they were poor. Simeon was a righteous and devout God-fearer in Jerusalem who was given a Holy Spirit-inspired vision that he would witness the long-awaited Messiah's coming (Luke 2:25-33), Israel's hope. As he holds the infant Jesus, he recognizes the true identity of this baby.

Simeon offers praise to God for finally sending the Messiah, a light for revelation to the Gentiles and glory to Israel (Isaiah 42:6-7, 46:13, 49:6). Simeon blesses Jesus' parents and turns to Mary with a somber message of coming intense opposition to her son and her own future suffering at his death. He predicts that Jesus is, "destined to cause the falling and rising of many in Israel, and to be a sign that will be spoken against" (Luke 2:34-25).

Anna, a godly Jewish prophetess from the tribe of Asher (Luke 2:36-38), was over one-hundred years old. Widowed after only seven years of marriage, she worshiped in the Jerusalem temple every day, morning and evening, praying and fasting. She is present when the baby Jesus is dedicated and recognizes his true identity as the Messiah. Her prophetic words, shared with those who were expectantly awaiting the "redemption of Jerusalem," revealed that Jesus is that redemption.

Q is for Quirinius

Administering the Census

The Roman Empire was established in 27 BC when Augustus became the sole ruler of Rome. It required great funds to support its military, building projects, and overall economy. Census taking was a common practice and used for administrative purposes in updating records. So the primary function of censuses was to determine how many people there were to tax.

The Roman government would set a fixed amount of money that each region was to provide in taxes. Local officials determined who should pay taxes and how much they should pay.

Quirinius was a successful Roman military commander, aristocrat, politician, administrator, and trusted associate of Caesar Augustus. The census mentioned in Luke 2:1-7, carried out by Herod the Great under Roman direction, was not the first census ever ordered, nor was it likely conducted by Quirinius; it was probably conducted prior to his time. This census, ordered by the conquering empire, required that the people return to the towns and villages of their ancestry. As Jews, Mary and Joseph were part of a conquered people group, so they were required to obey Roman rule.

Mary and Joseph, both being from the line of David, thus traveled from Nazareth to Bethlehem. God ordained Quirinius to be part of fulfilling ancient prophecy, responsible for Jesus' birth taking place in Bethlehem.

R is for Roman Rule

At the time of Jesus' birth, Rome held absolute power over its people. It was mighty, oppressive, and vast. Having quelled civil wars, rebellious provinces, and internal power struggles, Caesar Augustus was known as a "savior who has put an end to war."

Augustus' rule over Israel was administered through Herod the Great, who was also known as King Herod. Herod ruled the province of Judea at the time of Jesus' birth. He was known for his grand and numerous building accomplishments, as well as his paranoia. As a king appointed by Rome and living in luxury, Herod feared being exposed for his evil deeds and being deposed by a newborn baby, a supposed true king of noble Jewish descent. The announcement of a new king, let alone one of Jewish descent, was a threat to his power and authority.

Subjects of the Roman rule abhorred the enforced taxation, which was a sign of Rome's tyrannical, imperial power. While such taxation served to support the Roman government and military, it also served to remind the people of Judea they were bound to Rome. Amid heavy-handed Roman oppression and taxation, resentment and unrest among the Jewish people fueled insurrection and Jewish rebellions.

Because their beloved King David had been a warrior-king, the Jews expected their promised divine warrior-king to exercise his power in triumph over and against the oppression of foreign rulers. Unlike any previous king, however, this coming king and kingdom would reign forever (2 Samuel 7:12-13, 16).

S is for the Lowly Shepherds

The announcement of Jesus' birth was first proclaimed to a group of frightened shepherds in the fields nearby Bethlehem (Luke 2:8-9). Flocks of sheep that were kept for temple sacrifices in Jerusalem grazed in fields near Bethlehem throughout the year.

Shepherds lived a life in the fields committed to the care, provision, and protection of their sheep. Such protection was especially important at night, when thieves and predatory animals threatened the flock. Yet, because they tended sheep, they were rendered ritually unclean and considered among the lower class in Israel and were prevented from participating in religious activities.

That night, the shepherds experienced the sights and sounds of the angel's message and the great company of the heavenly host. Their collective response was to go in haste to find the newborn "Savior, who is Christ the Lord" (Luke 2:11). They would find him in the village, in a manger.

The Greek word, *kataluma*, translated "guest room" in Mark 14:14 and Luke 22:11, should be translated the same in Luke 2:7. First-century Palestinian homes typically consisted of one large family room where the household essentially lived. Sometimes a "guest room" was added to the home. Without available living space for Mary and Joseph in either the main house or the guest room, they stayed in a slightly lower-level part of the home where domesticated animals were kept.

The shepherds found the infant Jesus in a borrowed manger, a feeding trough of hewn stone used to hold food for the animals. The shepherds' presence at the birth of Jesus is evidence that the gospel (Good News) is for all people.

T is for the Perfect Moment in Time

When considering the timing of Jesus' birth, one might assume the relative, so-called peace of the *Pax Romana*, a safe, well-developed, and durable road system that facilitated travel and communication, or the dominance of one language (Common or Koine Greek) as reasons for the timeliness of Jesus' coming.

From God's salvation-historical perspective, however, the "fullness" or "completion" of time is measured according to his redemptive purposes (Galatians 4:4). It was the precise time when Israel and humanity were best prepared to receive the person and the work of Christ. In Jesus, God fulfills his irrevocable promise to Abraham that as the father of the nation of Israel, the world would be blessed through Abraham's descendants (Genesis 12:3). The time had come for the fulfillment of the prophetic expectation of Messiah's coming in salvation history. God sent his Son, Jesus, into our world, born like one of us, to be one of us, and to stand before God in our place. Divine timeliness is Jesus the Messiah coming not a moment too early nor a moment too late.

And as for the date of Jesus' birth, that is unknown. None of the Gospels directly address the issue. We do know, however, that Herod the Great died in 4 BC, according to the Gregorian calendar, the primary calendar used in the West today. Herod's edict to eliminate all the baby boys living in Bethlehem who were under two years old applied to those born between 6-4 BC.

U is for the Unveiled Prophecies

According to tradition, the first book of the Bible, Genesis, was written by Moses about 1,500 years before Christ was born. Early in Genesis, God begins to reveal his plan for sending the Savior. Just after Adam and Eve disobeyed God, he indicates that a victor would come from the seed of the woman, Eve (Gen 3:15). This seed, who is Jesus the Messiah, would be the one who would crush the head of the serpent.

God chooses Abraham and promises that He would make him into a great nation (Genesis 12:2-3). As part of that promise, God tells him that all people on earth will be blessed through him. This blessing is found in the One who redeems people from every tribe and tongue on earth. The blessing of salvation is for all who believe in the One sent and the Sender.

More than seven-hundred years before Jesus' birth, the prophet Isaiah wrote more than any other prophet about the Messiah, including his first coming. Isaiah records the character traits of the promised Messiah (Isaiah 9:6-7) through the following names. "Wonderful Counselor" describes the Savior as all-wise, offering counsel from God's perspective. "Mighty God" speaks of his unmatched strength because he is God. "Eternal Father" means that because He lives forever, His people will live forever. And "Prince of Peace" promises his ever-expanding, forever kingdom will be marked by a true and boundless peace. Isaiah then describes the king and His rule: He would come from the messianic line of David and would rule with justice and righteousness (Isaiah 9:7).

Jesus came, fulfilled, and continues to fulfill these prophecies, showing that God's promises are true.

V is for the Virgin Birth

Isaiah prophesied, "Therefore, the Lord Himself will give you a sign: The virgin will conceive, have a son, and name him Immanuel" (Isaiah 7:14). This is spoken to King Ahaz of Judah during a time of great political and military crisis, with the invading armies of Ephraim and Syria threatening his kingdom. As a short-term fulfillment, God assured Ahaz of his presence and deliverance from the impending war.

There is also a long-term fulfillment of the prophecy in this verse. A young woman, *almah* in Hebrew, will conceive and bear a son, whom she will name Immanuel. The Septuagint, the Greek translation of the Hebrew Bible, translates *almah* as *parthenos*, which typically means "a young woman of marriageable age." By the time Matthew wrote his Gospel, however, the word *parthenos* had come to mean "virgin" (Matthew 1:23). This shows us that God, the true author of Scripture, not only accurately predicts future events but is also sovereign over the development of language. God knew Isaiah 7:14 would be further fulfilled by Jesus' birth to a virgin.

Jesus' supernatural conception was by the Holy Spirit, the Third Person of the Trinity, who always carries out God's work. This means that the Messiah is fully God and fully human. He, then, is the only One able to serve as Mediator between God and man because he is both God and man.

W is for the Word of God

The apostle John emphasizes the theme of Jesus as "God with us" through his theological genealogy of Jesus, as opposed to Matthew (Matthew 1:1-17) and Luke's (Luke 3:23-38) biological genealogies (John 1:1-5). He states in verse 14, "The Word became flesh and dwelt among us, and we have seen his glory, glory as of the only Son from the Father, full of grace and truth." In this 'Word,' God fulfills his promise to come personally. God's divine glory takes on human flesh in human time and space. God came in the person of Jesus. The Incarnate Word of God, Jesus, is where the infinite and the finite exist together in the One who came.

The word John chooses for "dwelt" can be translated literally as "tabernacled." Jesus tabernacled among his people. When the reader or listener heard the word "tabernacled," they would be reminded of the portable tent where the Israelites met with God on their exodus from Egypt through the wilderness. This was where God resided with his people. Whenever they were commanded by God to rest and set up camp, the Tabernacle was always situated in the middle of their encampment, surrounded by the tribes of Israel. Sacrifices for the atonement of sin took place within, and through that sacrifice, corporate yet temporary cleansing was accomplished. Ultimate forgiveness of sin is now found completely and eternally in the God who tabernacles among us in human flesh, Jesus, the Word of God.

X is for Xmas

The letter "chi" (pronounced "key") is the 22nd of 24 letters of the Greek alphabet. "Chi" looks like the English letter "X" and is often used in the abbreviation "Xmas." Early Christians in ancient times used Greek abbreviations and "X" was common. The "X" in Xmas is thus not an "X" at all (as we understand it) but the Greek letter "chi," the first letter in the Greek title of *Christos* used for Jesus of Nazareth. It is not Jesus' last name but a title added to Jesus' proper name.

Christos means Christ, Anointed One, Sent One, or Savior of the world. The equivalent Hebrew word is *mashiach*, which becomes the English word, Messiah. Jews of the first century were expecting a Messiah who would deliver them from their Roman oppressors, as King David did from his enemies about a thousand years earlier. The Jews associated the Anointed One with the coming King from King David's line. As God's Anointed One, Messiah would conquer sin and its consequences, offering eternal life. As Messiah, Jesus fulfills God the Father's mission to deliver people from their sins.

When Herod summoned the chief priests and teachers of the law, he wanted to know where the Messiah (*Christos*) was to be born (Matthew 2:4). The "X" ("chi") in Xmas is a key part of the story of King Jesus' birth.

יֵשׁוּעַ

Yeshua

Salvation

Y is for Yeshua

The name, Jesus, is translated from the Hebrew Yeshua. The root of Jesus's name relates to the Hebrew word for *yeshuah*, which means, "to save," thus connecting his name with salvation. The title of Jesus is "Christ," from the Greek word, *Christos*. In the New Testament, *Christos* is frequently used in place of the Hebrew title, *Mashiach*, or Messiah, meaning "Anointed One." It is implied that the anointed one is sent from God. Thus, Jesus (Yeshua) is the Anointed One sent from God (*Mashiach*) into the world, providing salvation (*yeshuah*) to all who believe in him.

As the Bible explains, Messiah's coming would not be a temporal political move against enemies--even though this is what many Jews in that day expected-- but a transformative, spiritual revolution that would establish a new kingdom.

The angel Gabriel's words about Jesus to Joseph in his dream, "he will save his people from their sins," (Matthew 1:21) are both specific and significant. They reflect God's purpose and perspective, drawing attention to how this revolution will be accomplished. This Messiah will save those who respond and follow him—his people—from their sins.

Sin is anything that gets in the way of knowing God and living a reconciled relationship with him and others. It is a powerful, rebellious desire for independence from God and his ways that is found in each and every human being. Sin holds us captive; it is the work of the enemy. But Yeshua delivers us from the evil bondage of sin and sets us free. Our sin, then, is the cause of the perfectly sinless Yeshua's coming to provide *yeshuah*—salvation.

Z is for the Zeal

of the Shepherds

The night Jesus was born, there were shepherds in the fields outside Bethlehem caring for their flocks. They "kept watch," but it would be more accurate to say they were "keeping watches" (Luke 2:8). Shepherding was a 24/7 job, so they would take turns—some slept while others guarded the sheep. The constant threat of sheep stealing as well as attacks from preying animals required vigilance and alertness.

Together, these shepherds witness the angelic proclamation of Christ's coming. In response to the heavenly birth announcement, they excitedly seek and find the infant Child in the manger, just as had been told (Luke 2:12-20). They respond to all they see and hear by praising God, just as the angels had done. The Savior of the world has been born. The Messiah has arrived. His name is Jesus.

The shepherds marvel in amazement and cannot keep this good news to themselves. Rather, they make known the good news of God's gift to the world by telling others of their messianic encounter. And those who heard were also amazed. These shepherds were the first to proclaim Jesus' birth to their world and they did so with excitement and determination.

And just as the shepherds heard, heeded and headed out, so also those who choose to follow Christ are required to do the same. The good news proclaimed and fulfilled that night continues to be good news to many who hear it all over the world.

www.ingramcontent.com/pod-product-compliance
Lightning Source LLC
Chambersburg PA
CBHW041740160426
43200CB00003BA/34